The Portraits Of Vernon Hall

A Poetic Murder Mystery

Maanyatha Madhavan

/ BookLeaf
Publishing

India | USA | UK

Dedication

For those who have loved too deeply , and survived the storm.

Preface

*There are stories that begin with love, and end
with understanding.*
This is not one of them.

*At Vernon Hall, behind the ivy-curtained walls and gilded
portraits, love was never gentle. It was a slow, exquisite
undoing — a storm that carved the soul before it could calm
the sea.*

*What follows is a series of confessions — fragments of diary
pages, poems written in sleepless ink. Three voices echo
within these halls: a detective searching for truth, a man
haunted by devotion, and a girl whose love became her crime.*

*The Portraits of Vernon Hall is not merely a tale of a murder.
It is the anatomy of love — how it consumes, how it
manipulates, and how, in the end, it becomes the very thing
we destroy to save ourselves.*

Read carefully. Every verse is a clue, every silence a confession.

Acknowledgements

I owe this book to the quiet nights, multiple coffee runs, and the people who made me believe that even broken things can be beautiful and most importantly my parents who have always been by my side through my ups and downs (ilysm maa and papa <3)

To those who read my words and found a reflection of themselves — thank you for seeing me between the line.

Part A-The Investigation (Agatha Lorne)
1. The Bell at Midnight

The school bell rang twelve times that night.
It echoed through the halls, shaking the dust from the old ceilings.
By the time I reached the dormitory, the storm outside had gone quiet —
as if it too was breathing held.
A boy was on the floor next to his bed.
*His name was **Vernon.***
There was no glass, no blood,
just the expression of one who'd halted dreaming in mid-sentence.
*Someone breathed a girl's name — **Madea.***
And for some reason, that name lingered with me longer than the view of the body.

2. The Hallway Smells of Ink and Ash

The following morning, the corridor was filled with the scent of rain, decayed paper, and burnt something.
The students skirted the dorms, heads down, footwear squeaking against the wet floor.
The portraits on the walls appeared to observe all who walked by.
Vernon's desk was blanketed in doodles —
small hearts drawn in pen, a woman's initials looped beside his name.
There was still perfume in the air, sweet and gentle, but weighty.
Someone had loved too hard here.
And love, I've discovered, isn't always kind when it goes away.

3. A Note Beneath the Windowpane

They discovered a note under the window.
It was folded neatly, as if someone had considered
leaving it or destroying it.
The paper was soaked with rain.
The message read:
"You're the only warmth I have left."
The handwriting — tiny, precise, jumpy.
Initials at the end: M.D.
Madea.
The quiet one.
The girl who sits alone at the dinner table, writing when
no one's watching.
I know girls like her — the ones who love too much,
and lose themselves in it.

4. Madea's Handwriting

Her handwriting is tentative — as if she is scared of being misinterpreted.
Each line appears to be trying not to tremble.
The headmistress believes she's fragile.
The rest think she's odd.
Vernon used to refer to her as his muse.
I discovered her in the art room, in front of an incomplete portrait of him.
Her hands were spotless, but not her eyes.
When I asked her if she missed him, she replied, **"I loved him."**
And I believed her.
But it sounded more like a confession than love.

5. The Mirror in Vernon's Room

There's a mirror in Vernon's room — cracked straight down the middle.
On one, his smile; on the other, only a blur — perhaps her reflection once.
A lone ribbon rested on the ground at his elbow, neatly tied, unmarred by dust.
He'd scratched something light on the glass — her name, perhaps.
The candle next to it had burned all the way out.
Sometimes death doesn't enter in violence.
Sometimes, it enters quietly, and claims what's left of love.

Part B- The Lover's Diary (Vernon's Voice)
6. The Girl Who Spoke in Petals

She arrived at school in autumn.
Her bag was small, her eyes were still.
When she smiled, it seemed like sunlight in the elderly halls.
*All liked her, but she gazed **only at me.***
She uttered my name as if it pained her tongue — gentle, uncertain.
I appreciated it. I appreciated that she had to figure me out gradually.
She penciled in the margins of my books — flowers, mirrors, and sometimes my initials.
When she laughed, I was forgiven for everything.
I wrote her poems, slipped them under her door.
She kept each one, folded like prayers.
I thought that meant she'd stay.

7. Letters I Never Sent

I began writing to her at night, words I never dared to give her.
Things that sounded too heavy to say.
"You make me feel infinite."
"You make me jealous of the air around you."
Sometimes I tore them up after reading them out.
It wasn't love yet — not the way I wanted it.
I wanted her to see me as the reason she breathed.
When she hung out with others, I felt something twist inside.
*I told myself it was love. Maybe it was **hunger.***

8. When She Stopped Smiling

She's been quieter lately.
She still greets me at the lake, but she no longer takes my hand.
*She tells me **she's exhausted**, that the school is too much.*
I've told her I could make it lighter, that she doesn't have to share anything with anyone — just me.
She smiled weakly, though her eyes remained elsewhere.
She began writing in a new notebook.
I attempted to read it once, and she caught me.
Her expression — God, her expression — as if she'd seen something she couldn't unsee.
I apologized. She told me it's okay. It isn't.

9. The Garden Behind the Library

It's the only one that feels untouched.
The vines crawl up the wall like they're guarding secrets.
We used to sneak there after curfew, our shoes damp with dew.
She said she loved me there — once, softly, like **a confession she regretted**.
I told her she could not take it back. I said it as a joke, but she froze.
She said, **"Sometimes love feels like drowning."**
I laughed, but something inside of me cracked.
I began to dream of her walking out and never looking back.
I don't think I could handle that.

10. My Love, My Mirror

She's stopped talking much now.
I catch her staring at me as if she's memorizing it.
It frightens me — the softness of it.
I remind her she's all I have left, but she won't meet my
eyes.
When I reach out to touch her, she winces as if my hands
are burning.
I remind myself she's exhausted.
But sometimes I catch a glimpse of her in my window —
and it's not her I'm frightened of, it's the expression on
her face —
*as if **I'm the one she's buried already.***

Part C- The Becoming
(Madea's Voice)
11. I Sew My Heart Shut with Thread from His Tie

꧁✦꧂

I attempted to hold on to loving him like you hold a candle steady in the air.
Whenever it would sputter, I cupped my hands around it, and burned myself all over again.
He said he loved how quiet I was — so I learned to whisper even my thoughts.
He told me I completed him — so I started to unravel bit by bit.
He had a navy tie each Sunday; one time, I fantasized about its thread mending me whole.
*Today I realize **I was sewing a prison.***

12. The Night He Became Silent

It began raining early that night.
We had gathered in the library garden.
He spoke and spoke — of forever, of home.
I listened until words were heavy, until they rang like
chains.
He asked what had made me change.
*I explained to him, **"Because I can't breathe."***
He laughed quietly, as if I'd said something funny.
And then the air wasn't moving anymore.
The storm took the rest.
When I finally gazed downward, he wasn't speaking any
longer.

13. Agatha's Questions, My Calm Hands

They questioned where I was. I replied in the chapel, praying.
They inquired whether we'd fought. I informed them that we always did — quietly.
They gazed at my hands, as though guilt would flower there.
*But my hands were spotless. **All the filth was within me.***
When I returned to my room, his ribbon was on my pillow.
I used it to tie my hair back, and felt close.

14. What the Moon Saw Through the Window

~~~~

The moon observed me cleaning the mud from my boots.
It didn't judge. It's seen too many women scrub love out
of their skin.
I sat by the window and listened to the rain press its
fingers against the glass.
It whispered, **You're free.**
But freedom feels too much like silence.
I almost called his name, just to fill the room.

15. The Lake Remembers His Reflection

They dragged the lake for hours.
I stood at the dormitory steps, a tea cup trembling in my hand.
Each wave resembled him waving.
Agatha looked at me once, and I could tell she knew —
not how, not why —
but that love had misfired somewhere.
She said, "You were fond of him"
I said, "He made me happy."
It was true. And false.

16. His Scent in My Hair Like Sin

They say smell is memory.
Each time I braid my hair, his smell wafts up — the light cologne, the smoke, the ink.
I keep washing, but it lingers.
*Sometimes I think **it's not him I miss, but the girl who loved him.***
The girl who thought love was supposed to hurt a little.
Now, when I shut my eyes, I can almost hear him call my name —
as if he's asking me to finish the story.

17. The Fire in the Old Chapel

A candle was lit for him last night.
The wax oozed like blood across the altar.
I stood and watched the flame tremble, and wondered if that's how
his heart looked before it went still.
*I wanted to pray, but **my words kept turning into apologies**.*
The chapel air was flavored with smoke, and I knew the fire was growing.
I didn't step back. Some part of me wanted it to find me.

18. He Taught Me to Bleed Beautifully

*He once said **pain gives love its color.***
I believe that's why I stayed — to discover what color my heart would become.
He painted me with his words, until I'd resemble another.
When I finally shattered, it wasn't a scream — it was art.
People will say he died for love.
*They'll never understand **I was the one dying all along**.*

19. The Girl Who Spoke in Petals (Reprise)

I remember the first day once again — the autumn light,
the scent of ink, his laughter echoing down the hall.
He said that I spoke in petals.
He didn't know how easily petals bruise.
Now, as I walk past our old bench, the wind moves the
leaves like it's trying to talk for us.
I believe it's saying, ***"Both of you wanted to be loved.***
Only one of you learned how."

20. I Buried Him in My Smile

Everyone keeps saying I'm stronger now.
That I've healed.
I smile, and they believe it.
But sometimes I feel him in that smile — a small weight
behind my teeth.
He's buried in everything I do — the way I fold my
letters, the extinguishing of the light before bed.

Some ghosts don't haunt. They reside quietly within your
routines.

21. Madea's Final Letter to Agatha

Agatha,
by the time you read this, the roses will have bloomed again.
Their roots sip from the same soil that once contained him.
I want you to know — I didn't murder Vernon the boy.
I murdered Vernon the storm.
The one that rained until I drowned in my own mirror.
He was laughter, and ink, and the reason I forgot my name.
He was my joy, my prison, my downfall.
If love is a mirror, then I only shattered what reflected me.
Tell them he sleeps soundly.
Tell them I am finally still.
And if the wind blows through Vernon Hall tonight — listen.
It's only us, farewell, in the voice of the petals.